D1066065

Read-About® Health

How Does Your Brain Work?

By Don L. Curry

Consultants
Nanci R. Vargus, Ed.D.
Assistant Professor of Literacy
University of Indianapolis, Indianapolis, Indiana

Su Tien Wong
Professional Writer and Editor of Children's Books

Children's Press®
A Division of Scholastic Inc.
New York   Toronto   London   Auckland   Sydney
Mexico City   New Delhi   Hong Kong
Danbury, Connecticut

Designer: Herman Adler Design
Photo Researcher: Caroline Anderson
The photo on the cover shows a simple view of the brain.

Library of Congress Cataloging-in-Publication Data

Curry, Don L.
  How does your brain work? / Don L. Curry.– 1st American ed.
    p. cm. – (Rookie read-about health)
Includes index.
  ISBN 0-516-25859-1 (lib. bdg.)   0-516-27853-3 (pbk.)
  1. Brain–Juvenile literature. I. Title. II. Series.
  QP376.C87 2004
  612.8'2–dc21

                                        2003003912

Why can you read this book?

Why can you smile, see,
or talk?

You can do these things
and a lot more because
of your brain.

What is your brain?

Your brain is a wrinkly, soft, wet organ that is inside your skull.

Your skull is like a helmet made out of bones. Your skull protects your brain.

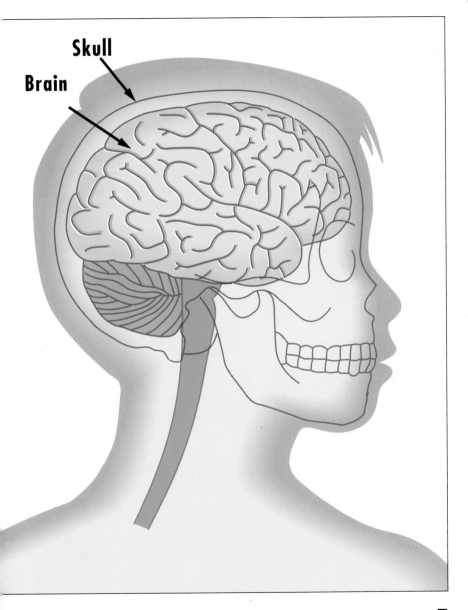

Skull

Brain

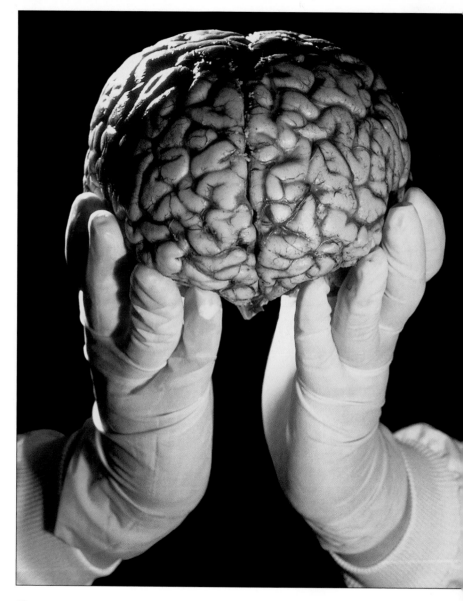

Your brain is not very big. It only weighs about 3 pounds. Someone could hold it in both hands.

Your brain stores what you learn so you can remember it later. This is called your memory.

Your brain is also where all
of your moods and feelings
come from.

Your brain tells different parts of your body what to do.

It tells your legs to move and your mouth to open.

13

Neuron branch

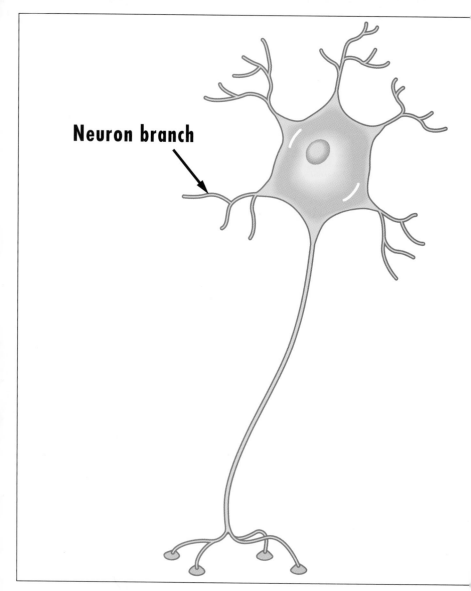

A neuron

Your brain may have as many as 100 billion (BIL-yuhn) neurons (NOO-rahnz) to do its work.

Neurons have branches, just like trees. The branches send messages to each other. Different parts of your body will receive the messages.

Your spinal cord runs down the middle of your back.

It sends messages from your brain to other parts of your body. It also takes messages from your body back to your brain.

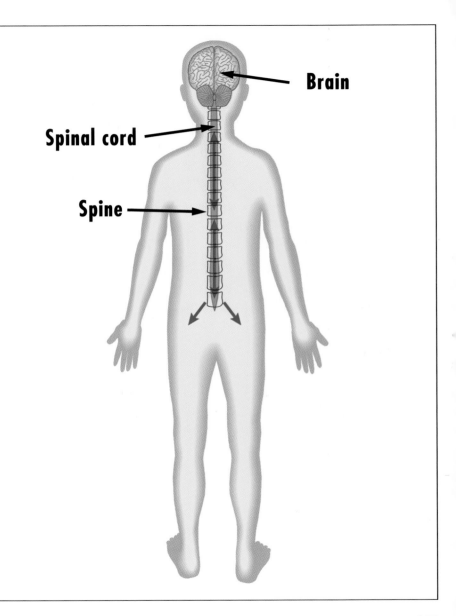

Brain

Spinal cord

Spine

Your brain is always busy.
It sends and receives
millions (MIL-yuhnz)
of messages every second
of every day.

This goes on all day and
all night, even while you
are sleeping.

Each part of your brain has a different job to do.

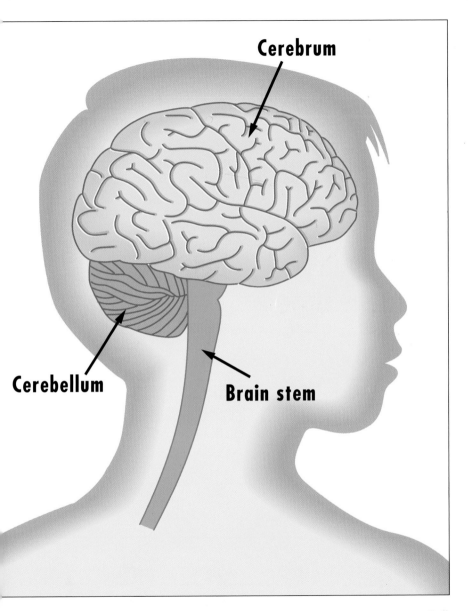

Cerebrum

Cerebellum

Brain stem

21

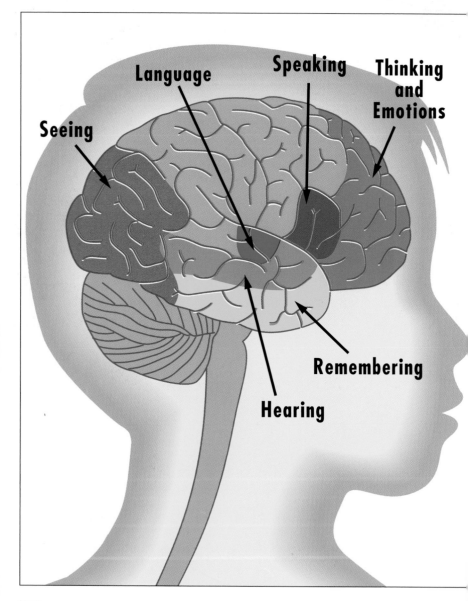

Seeing

Language

Speaking

Thinking and Emotions

Remembering

Hearing

The cerebrum (suh-REE-bruhm) is the biggest part of your brain. It controls things like seeing, hearing, speaking, thinking, and remembering.

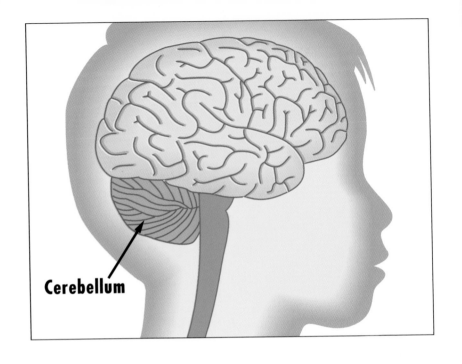

Cerebellum

Another important part of your brain is the cerebellum (SEH-ruh-BEL-uhm). The cerebellum controls your coordination.

This means that you can stand up or jump without falling down.

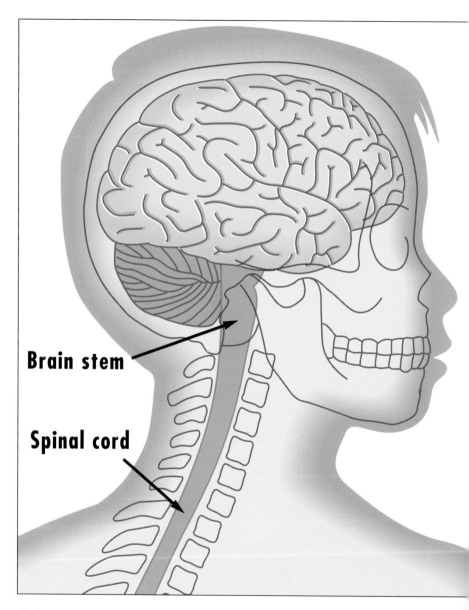

Brain stem

Spinal cord

Your brain stem
connects your brain
to your spinal cord.

Your brain stem makes
sure that you never have
to think about making
your heart beat, or
about breathing.

You need your brain to do almost everything.

In fact, right now your brain is sending a message telling your fingers to turn this page!

Words You Know

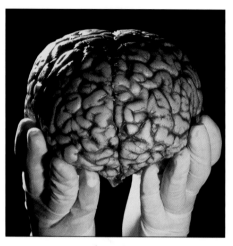

brain

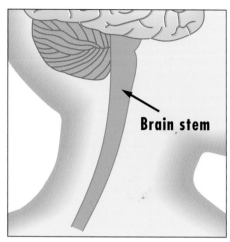

brain stem

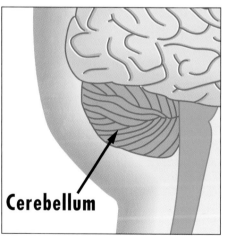

cerebellum

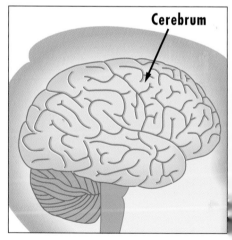

cerebrum

30

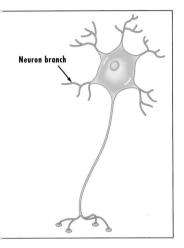

neuron

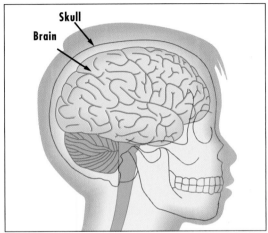

skull

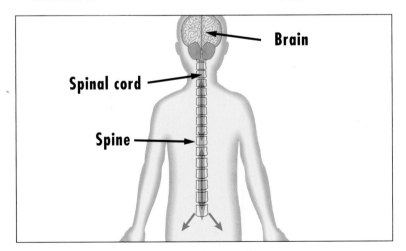

spinal cord

Index

About the Author

Don L. Curry is a writer, editor, and educational consultant who lives and works in New York City. When he is not writing, Don can generally be found in the park reading, or riding his bike exploring the streets of "the greatest city on Earth."

Photo Credits

Photographs © 2003: Peter Arnold Inc./Clyde H. Smith: 11; Photo Researchers, NY: 25 (Tim Davis), 8, 30 top left (Geoff Tompkinson/SPL); PhotoEdit: 10, 23 (Michael Newman), 4, 13 (David Young-Wolff); The Image Works: 18 (Esbin-Anderson), 29 (Steven Rubin); Visuals Unlimited/Robert Clay: 3.

Illustrations by Bob Italiano